CLOU... ...ESSES

M000074092

MARY
Favored by God

Catherine Upchurch

Little Rock
Scripture Study

A ministry of the Diocese of Little Rock
in partnership with Liturgical Press

Nihil obstat: Jerome Kodell, OSB, *Censor librorum*
Imprimatur: ✢ Anthony B. Taylor, Bishop of Little Rock, January 27, 2016

Contents

Introduction

Alive in the Word brings you resources to deepen your understanding of Scripture, offer meaning for your life today, and help you to pray and act in response to God's word.

Use any volume of **Alive in the Word** in the way best suited to you.

- **For individual learning and reflection,** consider this an invitation to prayerfully journal in response to the questions you find along the way. And be prepared to move from head to heart and then to action.
- **For group learning and reflection,** arrange for three sessions where you will use the material provided as the basis for faith sharing and prayer. You may ask group members to read each chapter in advance and come prepared with questions answered. In this kind of session, plan to be together for about an hour. Or, if your group prefers, read and respond to the questions together without advance preparation. With this approach, it's helpful to plan on spending more time for each group session in order to adequately work through each chapter.

- For a parish-wide event or use within a larger group, provide each person with a copy of this volume, and allow time during the event for quiet reading, group discussion and prayer, and then a final commitment by each person to some simple action in response to what he or she learned.

This volume explores the theme of **Cloud of Witnesses.** The pages of our Bibles are filled with the stories of women and men who have played a unique role in salvation history. By entering into a few key biblical passages written by or describing these people, we begin to see how our own story continues God's great work of salvation in the world. Their witness, handed on to us from centuries ago, continues to speak to us and challenge us to stand as faithful witnesses in today's world.

The Annunciation

Begin by asking God to assist you in your prayer and study. Then read through Luke 1:26-38, the story of the annunciation of the birth of Jesus.

Luke 1:26-38

26In the sixth month, the angel Gabriel was sent from God to a town of Galilee called Nazareth, 27to a virgin betrothed to a man named Joseph, of the house of David, and the virgin's name was Mary. 28And coming to her, he said, "Hail, favored one! The Lord is with you." 29But she was greatly troubled at what was said and pondered what sort of greeting this might be. 30Then the angel said to her, "Do not be afraid, Mary, for you have found favor with God. 31Behold, you will conceive in your womb and bear a son, and you shall name him Jesus. 32He will be great and will be called Son of the Most High, and the Lord God will give him the throne of David his father, 33and he will rule over the house of Jacob forever, and of his kingdom there will be no end." 34But Mary said to the angel, "How can this be, since I have no relations with a man?" 35And the angel said to her in reply, "The holy Spirit will come upon you, and the power of the Most High will overshadow you. Therefore the child to be born will be called holy, the Son of God. [36]And behold, Elizabeth, your relative, has also conceived a son in her old age, and this is the sixth month for her who was called barren; [37]for nothing will be impossible for God." [38]Mary said, "Behold, I am the handmaid of the Lord. May it be done to me according to your word." Then the angel departed from her.

> *After a few moments of quiet reflection on the scene, consider the information provided in "Setting the Scene."*

Setting the Scene

The Gospel of Luke is dominated by a journey motif or theme, with significant events seeming to occur in logical order as the reader moves with the action toward Jerusalem and the events of Jesus' passion, death, and resurrection. Even this first chapter of the gospel account unfolds in an orderly way, with the announcement of the birth of John the Baptist (1:5-25), the forerunner of Jesus, occurring before the announcement of the birth of Jesus.

John's parents, Elizabeth and Zechariah, serve as a type of bridge between the Old and New Testaments. Both are descendants of the priestly clans of Israel and described as "righteous in the eyes of God" (1:5-6). We may assume that, as righteous people, the law of God was their anchor, and faithfulness to God's word their way of conducting themselves in the world. Later in the gospel, the Roman centurion who witnesses the crucifixion will declare Jesus to be righteous

Righteousness may be described as being in right relationship with God. In your life, who models this kind of righteousness for you?

(23:47, also translated as "innocent"). Joseph of Arimathea, who claimed his broken body, is also described as a "righteous man" (23:50).

This elderly couple epitomized the best of faithful Israel, and yet Elizabeth had remained childless. Such a fate was often seen as an embarrassment or even a judgment on a woman's morality. Having been described as "righteous," Elizabeth's barrenness had nothing to do with her spiritual state. Her pregnancy is undoubtedly the stuff of miracles—God intervening in totally unexpected and seemingly impossible ways.

From the old and foundational comes something new and fresh, and it is this direction that Luke the evangelist pursues as he describes the encounter between the angel Gabriel and a young Jewish girl named Mary.

Understanding the Scene Itself

The entire passage will be considered a few verses at a time. The occasional questions in the margin (as above) are for discussion with others. If you are using these materials on your own, use the questions for personal reflection or as a guide to journaling.

26In the sixth month, the angel Gabriel was sent from God to a town of Galilee called Nazareth, 27to a virgin betrothed to a man named Joseph, of the house of David, and the virgin's name was Mary.

Referencing "the sixth month" is a connection to the previous story of good news for Elizabeth and Zechariah, again connecting the two pregnancy events much as the two sons in their adult lives will be connected in public memory.

The particular angel sent to Mary (and in the previous story to Zechariah) is Gabriel, known in Jewish tradition from the eighth chapter of the book of Daniel, where he interpreted a vision of the end-times when God would sit in judgment of the wicked. After hearing Gabriel's interpretation, the prophet Daniel is said to have been left weak and ill for several days, even "desolate" at the news of such judgment (Dan 8:27). One can only imagine how a young girl generations later, familiar with her religious tradition of which Gabriel is a part, might have felt upon encountering Gabriel himself.

The scene takes place in a particular location, Nazareth. This town is not directly mentioned in the Old Testament, in spite of the reference in the Gospel of Matthew (2:23) that the prophets said, "He shall be called a Nazorean." Some scholars believe Matthew's note is a play on the word *neṣer*, meaning "shoot," as in the shoot of Jesse (Isa 11:1). In the Gospel of Luke, Nazareth is the home of Joseph and Mary, and the location of Jesus' childhood home.

Located about halfway between the Sea of Galilee and the Mediterranean Sea, Nazareth is near the lower end of the Lebanon mountain range, approximately sixty-five miles north of Jerusalem. (See the map on page 40.) Although little is known of this town at the time of Jesus, Luke records that Gabriel's annunciation to Mary occurred there. This is also the location of the famous scene that begins the public ministry of Jesus as he reads from the scroll of Isaiah in the synagogue and proclaims, "Today this scripture passage is fulfilled in your hearing" (Luke 4:16-21).

Basilica of the Annunciation

Today Nazareth is a rather large city that includes a number of noted churches, two of which relate to the events of the first chapter of Luke. Saint Joseph's Church, containing ruins from the first century, is revered as the workshop of Joseph (described as a carpenter in Matt 13:55) and the home of the Holy Family. The Basilica of the Annunciation, completed in 1969, memorializes the encounter between Mary and the angel Gabriel described in the first chapter of Luke. As the largest church in the Middle East, the basilica is frequented by international tourists who wish to worship there and meditate on the numerous depictions of Mary from all parts of the world.

God worked within Mary's life circumstances in Nazareth. How might God be working in your own circumstances at this time in your life?

In Luke's telling of the story, he says simply, "the virgin's name was Mary" (1:27), a name from the tradition of Miriam, sister of Moses and Aaron, a name meaning "sea of bitterness and sorrow." Mary is described as a virgin who is betrothed to a man named Joseph. In this culture, betrothal was a formal agreement of marriage, the marriage itself beginning once the young woman was physically mature enough to become pregnant. Given that Mary is not yet living with Joseph, we may assume that she was still too physically immature to bear a child. This sets the stage for God's intervention in her life.

Joseph is "of the house of David," indicating Jesus' connection to the everlasting dynasty promised to David: "Your house and your kingdom are firm forever before me; your throne shall be firmly established forever" (2 Sam 7:16).

[28]And coming to her, he said, "Hail, favored one! The Lord is with you." [29]But she was greatly troubled at what was said and pondered what sort of greeting this might be. [30]Then the angel said to her, "Do not be afraid, Mary, for you have found favor with God."

Unlike Zechariah who was a priest serving at the temple when he received the news of Elizabeth's pregnancy, Mary was simply a young woman living in an obscure village. And yet Gabriel's first words to Mary tell us immediately and directly that she is among those favored by God. Why would this message have troubled Mary? The Greek term *charis* and Hebrew *hēn* may both be translated as "favor" or "grace." In the Jewish tradition it generally means that God is positively disposed to the person, though this should not be confused with receiving special treatment or favoritism.

Mary surely wondered how she could be counted among those receiving divine favor. Consider some in the Jewish tradition who are said to have been favored by God: Noah (Gen 6:8);

> When have you been fearful of God or the promptings of God?

> How has God's promise to be present with us helped to put your fears into perspective?

Joseph (Gen 39:20-23); Moses (Exod 33:12-13); Hannah (1 Sam 2:21) and her son, Samuel the prophet (1 Sam 2:26). In each of these cases, the characters are charged with difficult tasks—from preserving creation from destruction, to taking charge of royal duties, to leading people out of slavery, to speaking God's word to those who find it difficult to hear. Being favored by God usually came with great responsibilities. But it also came with the reassurance that there is nothing to fear.

[31]"Behold, you will conceive in your womb and bear a son, and you shall name him Jesus. [32]He will be great and will be called Son of the Most High, and the Lord God will give him the throne of David his father, [33]and he will rule over the house of Jacob forever, and of his kingdom there will be no end."

Now Gabriel's message takes on the particular way in which Mary will experience God's favor. She will conceive and bear a son. In the Old Testament tradition, two women were visited by an angel and told they would bear sons, men who played significant roles in salvation history. One woman was Hagar, Sarah's maid and the woman who would bear Abraham's first son, Ishmael. The Lord's angel appeared to Hagar when she ran away to the desert (Gen 16:7-13) and announced that her descendants would be numerous, specifically, "You are now pregnant and shall bear a son; / you shall name him Ishmael." The other woman was the previously barren mother of Samson to whom an angel of the Lord said, "Though you are barren and have had no children, you will conceive and bear a son" (Judg 13:1-5). Samson would be one of Israel's leaders who wielded power against Israel's enemies, the Philistines.

The name and titles of Mary's child recorded in Luke reveal that the child is the fulfillment of all of Israel's hopes, as this passage makes use of language that is typically associated with God's presence and power to act on Israel's behalf.

The name "Jesus" means simply "the Lord saves," a clear proclamation of God's overarching purpose. Just as the psalmists (e.g., Ps 48:2; 86:10; 96:4) acclaim that God is great and mighty, Gabriel indicates this child will grow up to be "great." In Israel's tradition, those who are called by God and remain faithful are sometimes referred to as sons of God, and the "Most High" is a clear reference to God. Israel's kings were also designated as sons of God (e.g., 2 Sam 7:14; Ps 2:7; 89:28). And finally, the promise to David that his kingdom would be established forever (2 Sam 7:13-17) is brought to fulfillment in this promise to give Mary's child "the throne of David."

Luke focuses on the names and titles for Jesus that connect with Israel's expectations. What titles for Jesus do you most often use in prayer? Why?

³⁴But Mary said to the angel, "How can this be, since I have no relations with a man?" ³⁵And the angel said to her in reply, "The holy Spirit will

come upon you, and the power of the Most High will overshadow you. Therefore the child to be born will be called holy, the Son of God. [36]And behold, Elizabeth, your relative, has also conceived a son in her old age, and this is the sixth month for her who was called barren; [37]for nothing will be impossible for God."

Mary's response reveals her humanity as she tells Gabriel that a pregnancy is not possible because her marriage is not consummated and, in fact, she has never had sexual relations. More important in the way Luke weaves his story is the connection to Israel's hopes for a promised Messiah to be born of an Israelite virgin (Isa 7:14). This is not an ordinary reporting of the facts but opens the way for a profound promise and the first appearance in Luke's gospel of the Spirit of God.

It is the gift of God's Spirit who not only brings about the birth of Jesus, but also plays a significant role throughout the Gospel of Luke and Luke's second volume, the Acts of the Apostles.

In Luke's accounts, it is the Spirit who

Where do you see evidence that the Spirit of God is still at work in our world?

- reveals the significance of Jesus' birth to Simeon (Luke 2:25ff.);
- descends on Jesus at his baptism (Luke 3:22);
- accompanies Jesus in the desert at the time of his temptation (Luke 4:1);
- animates Jesus from the start of his public ministry (Luke 4:18-21);

- becomes a divine gift to Jesus' followers (Luke 11:13; Acts 1:8-9; 2:1-4, 33; 10:44);
- teaches Jesus' followers how to respond to opposition (Luke 12:10-12; Acts 7:54-60);
- equips Jesus' followers to preach throughout the region (Acts 13:1-4; 19:21-22).

Gabriel tells Mary, "The holy Spirit will come upon you, and the power of the Most High will overshadow you." Similar words are spoken to the followers of Jesus gathered together after Jesus' death and resurrection: "you will receive power when the holy Spirit comes upon you" (Acts 1:8). In the latter case, the church is being equipped for the mission from Jerusalem to the ends of the earth. In the former case, Mary is being told that her mission to bear the "Son of the Most High" will be the work of God's own Spirit within her. It is not human power but God's power that will overshadow Mary as she begins this mission.

How would you describe the activity of God's Spirit in your own life?

Again, some background might help communicate how Mary heard these words about being overshadowed. In the heart of the Jewish tradition is the experience of the exodus from Egypt, with the accompanying wandering in the desert and making a covenant with God. Consider that Moses, drawn to a burning bush while shepherding sheep, experiences a revelation of God, an encounter that he surely believed would overwhelm or even destroy him and so he hid his face (Exod 3:1-6). As the liberated slaves made their way toward the Promised Land, God's presence overshadowed them in the form of a pillar of cloud by day and a pillar of fire by night (Exod 13:21-22). God's presence was both overwhelming and comforting. Being overshadowed by God's presence and power could have left Mary experiencing both as well. Like the prophets before her, overshadowed by God's presence and empowered to speak God's word, Mary will also bear God's Word to the world.

The next verses (1:36-37) move Mary, and us, further into the realm of religious imagination, not as a flight of fancy but as an invitation to embrace something much greater than logic would allow. God has intervened to allow a barren relative to conceive a child. Here again there is a connection of sorts to the previous story of Elizabeth's pregnancy. On one end of the spectrum, Elizabeth is too elderly to conceive and bear a child, and on the other end, Mary is too young and is not married. Has Gabriel finally captured her imagination? Is this announcement about Elizabeth the sign that Mary needs to assure her of God's call and gift, and her unique role in salvation history?

"[F]or nothing will be impossible for God" is another phrase that both serves Israel's memory and promises a new future. When Sarah overheard the news given to Abraham that she would bear a child (Gen 18:9-15), she laughed, causing the Lord to say to her husband, "Is anything too marvelous for the LORD to do?" Now, in the

Are you able to identify with Mary's response to Gabriel? How so?

Is there an "impossible" situation that you would like to ask God to transform?

announced pregnancy of Elizabeth, the angel invites Mary to enter into that same sense of wonder and awe in the face of God's power and generosity. She is now ready to respond to God's plan, to choose to put herself at the service of this God who intervenes in history and whose promises are worthy of trust.

38Mary said, "Behold, I am the handmaid of the Lord. May it be done to me according to your word." Then the angel departed from her.

Mary's response to God's plan, translated as it is in our own language, sometimes sounds so docile as to be passive. Perhaps this impression is further complicated by the fact that so much art over the centuries, as profoundly beautiful as it may be, depicts Mary with her eyes downcast and her head tilted in submission. But we must be careful not to confuse resignation or a sense of unworthiness with true humility.

The Latin root of "humility" is derived from the word *humus*, the term that applies to the earth. We could say that Mary is of the earth, grounded in her identity. Mary is a "handmaid of the Lord," much as Hannah, the mother of Samuel, was a handmaid and servant who prayed for a son (1 Sam 1:11). Mary knows her place in relationship to God and therefore she knows that she can be of service. This is the time that her service is needed. Far from passive, she is actively responding to God's plan and embracing her role.

Perhaps it would serve us well to see her response to God's plan in light of another response in Israel's history. When Moses heard his name called from the burning bush, he uttered a simple word, "*Hineni!*" meaning "Here I am." In the context of that event described in Exodus 3, Moses is not simply answering to his name; he is placing himself at God's service, ready to be given a commission. Similarly, Mary is placing herself in service to God's plan, even as unbelievable as it sounds to her.

Her *fiat* (Latin, meaning "let it be done") reminds us that we may freely choose to reject or to participate in God's life in us, and God's movements in our world. In Mary's case, a young woman from a small village, someone who would have been considered a bit marginal, is now front and center in the plan of God, not just for her own life but for the life of the world. She said "yes," trusting in God's will and power to create life, even though she could not have known completely what it would mean for her or her family.

> Consider how and when you have been aware of saying "yes" to what God has in store for you. Did consenting to God's plan call forth a greater ability to trust God in other areas of your life?

Praying the Word / Sacred Reading

Return to the passage in Luke 1:26-38, reading it deliberately and prayerfully. Consider what words or phrases stand out for you and spend a bit of time rolling these words and phrases over in your heart. If you are sharing this with a group, allow for some quiet time, and then talk about the various pieces of this passage that stand out for each of you.

Place yourself in the position of Mary, perhaps looking back at this time in her life when the whole world changed for her. If the following words help you to do that, then use them as your own prayer or as a group prayer, or feel free to create your own prayerful reflection on the scene by placing yourself in her position.

When I was just a young girl,
barely old enough to call myself a woman,
you, O God, sent an angel to visit me.
I was innocent and couldn't know what you
    had in mind
but I did know the stories of my people,
and I recognized that Gabriel's mere presence
    could be foreboding.
Why, of all the angels, would you send Gabriel,
the interpreter of frightening signs from the
    time of Daniel?
Would this be a frightening time for me?

Why would Gabriel tell me that I was favored?
Isn't that the same message that came to our
    great prophets?
Your "favor" seemed to get them in all kinds
    of hot water.
And weren't our kings favored too?

It seemed to me that to be favored
could lead to places that troubled me—
being called upon to speak on your
        behalf,
being asked to act as you would act,
being misunderstood,
being rejected—
To be favored was not simply a privilege,
it was a responsibility.

"Do not be afraid" were the sweetest words I
        could have heard.

You, God, were in charge,
    and would use my pondering,
    and my confusion,
    and my joyful consent
to do something beautiful in me,
something beautiful for all generations!

Living the Word

Consider some tangible way you may help someone you know hear God's words, "Be not afraid," in their own life situation. Is there something you can do to demonstrate your willingness to be with someone in need of courage? Can your presence with another person be a confirmation of God's desire to accompany that person through a fearful time?

The Visitation

Statue at Church of the Visitation

Begin by asking God to assist you in your prayer and study. Then read through Luke 1:39-45, the story of the visitation, when Mary travels from Nazareth to the hill country to be with Elizabeth.

Luke 1:39-45

³⁹During those days Mary set out and traveled to the hill country in haste to a town of Judah, ⁴⁰where she entered the house of Zechariah and greeted Elizabeth. ⁴¹When Elizabeth heard Mary's greeting, the infant leaped in her womb, and Elizabeth, filled with the holy Spirit, ⁴²cried out in a loud voice and said, "Most blessed are you among women, and blessed is the fruit of your womb. ⁴³And how does this happen to me, that the mother of my Lord should come to me? ⁴⁴For at the moment the sound of your greeting reached my ears, the infant in my womb leaped for joy. ⁴⁵Blessed are you who believed that what was spoken to you by the Lord would be fulfilled."

After a few moments of quiet reflection on the passage, consider the background information provided in "Setting the Scene."

21

Setting the Scene

With this scene we travel a distance of about ninety miles between Nazareth and the Judean hill country, between the area around the Sea of Galilee and the region around Jerusalem. (See the map on page 32.)

The village associated for many centuries with the visitation is known today as Ein Kerem and is located just a few miles southwest of the capital city of Jerusalem. In the lower portion of the town pilgrims today can visit the Church of St. John the Baptist, which encloses a grotto venerated as the spot of John's birth. The walls of the surrounding courtyard contain tiles of the Canticle of Zechariah in many languages. This same canticle, upholding God's power to save all through Jesus Christ, is prayed across the world for Morning Prayer as part of the Liturgy of the Hours.

Church of the Visitation

Just above the town itself, the Church of the Visitation is perched on a picturesque hillside, commemorating the site where two women, chosen by God, greeted one another with joyful news that would change the world. From this vantage point the roughly terraced hillsides give evidence of the ingenuity of ancient farmers who found ways to use a somewhat daunting terrain for their most basic needs.

Understanding the Scene Itself

> The entire passage will be considered a few
> verses at a time. The occasional questions in
> the margin may be used in group discussion or
> for your own personal reflection.

³⁹**During those days Mary set out and traveled
to the hill country in haste to a town of Judah,
⁴⁰where she entered the house of Zechariah and
greeted Elizabeth.**

The "haste" of Mary's journey to be with
Elizabeth was more a matter of spiritual urgency
than a matter of fact. Such a journey would not
have been undertaken without some planning. A
young girl in first-century Palestine would not
have traveled by herself even to a nearby location, and certainly not a distance of ninety miles,
without an escort and some planning for safe
travel. Saying she went in haste is perhaps more
a reflection on Mary's swift reaction to share the
news. She doesn't linger in doubt or confusion
but moves forward, confident that she is part of
a larger sacred mystery.

In this simple scene of the two women coming
together, there are a number of suggestions to
help modern Bible readers see the scene in its
richness. Beyond the mere improbability of these
two bearing children without God's intervention, there are other layers of meaning to be
uncovered here.

It could be said that Elizabeth represents the
former covenant and Mary the new covenant,

embracing here, their wombs between them carrying John and Jesus. It is as if two times of God's pronounced presence have come together and the lynchpin is Jesus, bringing God's covenant to fullness.

It also has been observed that in Luke's writings he sometimes brings together two people whose individual religious experiences may not yet be fully understood. Their actual time together often reveals more fully how God is at work within them. For example, in the Acts of the Apostles, also written by Luke, consider these scenes:

When has sharing a religious experience with someone else helped you to understand and embrace it more fully?

Did this sharing come about by unplanned circumstances or by your desire and design?

- Philip and the Ethiopian eunuch (Acts 8:26-40) meet while traveling through Samaria. In their sharing Philip sees that God has plans beyond the mission to Israel, while the Ethiopian moves from godly devotion to the full faith of baptism.
- Saul and Ananias (Acts 9:1-19) meet after Saul has experienced the risen Christ and has been blinded. Through their meeting, Ananias learns the surprising result of obedience to God's promptings, while Saul receives the gift of restored sight and the Holy Spirit to guide him on an unexpected mission to the Gentiles.
- Peter and the Roman centurion Cornelius (Acts 10:1-49) are brought together after both men receive visions and have to be willing to pursue a plan that might have seemed unlikely. In the end, Peter discovers that God shows no partiality and Cornelius and his

household receive the faith through an outpouring of the Holy Spirit and baptism.

⁴¹When Elizabeth heard Mary's greeting, the infant leaped in her womb, and Elizabeth, filled with the holy Spirit, ⁴²cried out in a loud voice and said, "Most blessed are you among women, and blessed is the fruit of your womb. ⁴³And how does this happen to me, that the mother of my Lord should come to me? ⁴⁴For at the moment the sound of your greeting reached my ears, the infant in my womb leaped for joy."

This scene is permeated with joy and a sense of presence. The women are totally present to one another and to this moment of God's intervention in their lives. This is not a gathering of shame or embarrassment, not a time of worry or confusion, but a time of expectation, literally and figuratively.

What does it mean to be called blessed? In the Hebrew tradition a blessing is a share in God's life. In the creation story of Genesis 1, God blessed the humans made in his image, giving them power to fill the earth (1:28). Made in the image of the Creator God, humans share in the creative process. Also in Genesis, God tells Abram that he will "be a blessing" (12:1-3), that

Pope Francis reminds us that the Gospel invites us to "run the risk of face-to-face encounters with others" partly to hear their pain and partly to be infected with joy from each other (The Joy of the Gospel, #88). Mary and Elizabeth share just such a moment. How does this very human encounter speak to you?

in and through him God's covenant will spread throughout the earth.

A blessing is also a source of happiness. "Blessed are you" can be understood as "happy are you." Luke 6 clearly has this in mind by closing the beatitudes with "Rejoice and leap for joy on that day!" (6:23). In the scene with the two pregnant women it is the child in Elizabeth's womb who leaps for joy as he and his mother recognize God's blessing.

The double mention of Elizabeth's child leaping in the womb (1:41, 44) would have drawn a religiously significant parallel for Jews who knew their ancestral stories. Many scholars suggest that Luke wrote this in a way that would call to mind the story of the twins Esau and Jacob, who "jostled" in the womb of Rebekah (Gen 25:21-23). In that ancient scene God told Rebekah that "the older will serve the younger," explaining the reversal of roles between Esau and Jacob. Now the implication for Elizabeth and Mary is that the older of these two boys, John, will serve the younger, Jesus.

Elizabeth's words, "Most blessed are you among women, and blessed is the fruit of your womb," show that she is filling a prophetic role in the scene, recognizing and identifying what God is doing. She acknowledges Mary's chosen status as an instrument of God. And further, she proclaims the fruit of Mary's womb to be "my Lord."

Elizabeth is the first to proclaim Jesus' identity, even before his birth. Her son John will echo her words in his ministry, preparing the way of

the Lord with a baptism for re-
pentance. When asked if he was
the awaited Messiah, John re-
plied, "one mightier than I is
coming. I am not worthy to
loosen the thongs of his sandals"
(Luke 3:16). Both Elizabeth and
John knew God's action in their
lives, but were humble enough
to recognize that in Mary and
Jesus something definitive was
happening. God was breaking
into the world in a new way.

45 "Blessed are you who believed that what was
spoken to you by the Lord would be fulfilled."

When we come right down to it, Elizabeth is
acknowledging the powerful act of trust that
brought Mary to say yes to God's plan. It was
not an act of the intellect to believe that God
would be true to his word. It was an act of trusting that God was worthy of such surrender. It
involved all that it is to be human—her body,
mind, and soul. Elizabeth is also applauding the
action of God in her young kinswoman.

There is, however, a larger picture here when
speaking of the Lord's word being fulfilled. This
is not merely about God's word to a young virgin in Nazareth, but in truth is about the word
of salvation God promised throughout salvation
history. In many ways, Mary represents the
people of God who have waited expectantly for
God's continued, and now definitive, action on
their behalf.

The root word
for "humility"
and "human" is
humus, meaning
"earth" or
"ground."
Humility does
provide a
grounding for
our experience
as humans.
When have you
witnessed the
power of
someone
exhibiting true
humility?

What things
challenge your
willingness to
trust God?

What things have
helped you to
grow in trusting
God?

God's covenant word to Abraham to provide an abundance of descendants (Gen 12:1-3; 15:1-6) prepared for this moment. In this new time those descendants would not be restricted to the clans and tribes of Israel but would include all peoples. God's word to Moses and the Hebrews to make them his people (Lev 26:12) would now extend to all the peoples of the earth. God's word to King David to establish an everlasting throne (2 Sam 7:16) will be realized in the offer of everlasting life. All made possible by God's word spoken to a young maiden and the birth of a child who will be revealed as Lord.

Praying the Word / Sacred Reading

Return to the full passage of the visitation in Luke 1:39-45. Read it slowly and prayerfully in full. What phrases or sentences speak to you? Linger with these phrases as you allow God to work within you.

Perhaps these words will assist you in further prayer:

Like Mary, may I create the opportunity to
    share good news,
    embrace a new thing God is doing even when
        it seems impossible,
        and receive God's word with joyful accep-
           tance.

Like Elizabeth, may I recognize the presence of
    God in and around me,
    foster in my family the desire to proclaim
        good news,

and humbly fulfill the plan of God in my
own life.

Living the Word

*Who might delight in a visit from you? How
might your presence with someone at this time
become a sign of God's presence and care? Consider some practical ways that you might share
joy and good news with others, especially in a
world where it seems so little good news occu-
pies the headlines.*

The Canticle of Mary

After asking God to assist you in your prayer and study, slowly read through Luke 1:46-55, the Canticle of Mary (also known as the Magnificat*).*

Luke 1:46-55

[46]And Mary said:

"My soul proclaims the greatness of the Lord;
    [47]my spirit rejoices in God my savior.
[48]For he has looked upon his handmaid's lowliness;
    behold, from now on will all ages call me blessed.
[49]The Mighty One has done great things for me,
    and holy is his name.
[50]His mercy is from age to age
    to those who fear him.
[51]He has shown might with his arm,
    dispersed the arrogant of mind and heart.
[52]He has thrown down the rulers from their thrones
    but lifted up the lowly.
[53]The hungry he has filled with good things;
    the rich he has sent away empty.

⁵⁴He has helped Israel his servant,
  remembering his mercy,
⁵⁵according to his promise to our fathers,
  to Abraham and to his descendants forever."

Setting the Scene

> After a few moments of quiet reflection on the passage, consider the background information provided in "Setting the Scene."

A canticle is simply a song, poem, or hymn that gives praise to God. Many such hymns are found throughout the Bible, with a few of them from Luke's gospel finding their way into the official daily prayer of the church, known as the Liturgy of the Hours:

- The Canticle of Zechariah (Luke 1:68-79) is found in Morning Prayer.
- The Canticle of Simeon (Luke 2:29-32) is found in Night Prayer.
- The Canticle of Mary (above) is found in Evening Prayer.

Prayerfully read through each of the canticles found in the Gospel of Luke. Why do you suppose the church recommends that these prayers become our own? How can you relate to them?

Each of these canticles captures something essential about Christian faith: Zechariah's is a proclamation of God's power acting through Jesus Christ to save the world, Simeon's expresses gratitude for having witnessed the fulfillment of God's promise, and Mary's models and invites surrender to God's will working in our world and our individual lives.

It is important for modern readers to remember that the gospels were not on-the-spot reporting but testimonies of faith. While it is unlikely that Mary actually composed these words at the time of her visit with Elizabeth, there is no doubt that the well-crafted words of this hymn reflect what the early followers of Christ saw in her life as both the mother of Jesus and his disciple.

The gospels are first and foremost testimonies of faith.

Much like the very pregnancy of Mary, this prayer invites us to move beyond the rational or the logical so that we can enter into the place where indeed all things are possible with God. The words on the lips of Mary are a bit like taking a peek into her prayer journal or entering into the pondering and reflecting that Luke later notes after the birth of Jesus (Luke 2:19).

The wording of Mary's canticle borrows from many Old Testament references, especially the Psalms. Her prayer is also reminiscent of the prayer of Hannah after the long-awaited birth of her son (1 Sam 2:1-10). Both women acclaim God's action in their lives, acknowledge God's power to destroy enemies, and proclaim a reversal of fortune for the poor and lowly.

Understanding the Scene Itself

> *The entire passage will be considered a few verses at a time. The occasional questions in the margin may be used in group discussion or for your own personal reflection.*

[46]And Mary said:
"My soul proclaims the greatness of the Lord;
   [47]my spirit rejoices in God my savior.
[48]For he has looked upon his handmaid's lowliness;
   behold, from now on will all ages call me blessed.
[49]The Mighty One has done great things for me,
   and holy is his name."

The prayer opens with Mary's personal experience of God and reveals that she has a sense of her own purpose in God's plan. She is both lowly *and* blessed, which gives her great joy (a recurring theme throughout the Gospel of Luke). All is due not to her worthiness but to God's generosity.

This pattern of God seeking out the lowly and bypassing those with more obvious status is a pattern that will be repeated often throughout the Gospel of Luke. Mary's lowliness can rightly be attributed to her young age, her gender, and her lack of political power. However, her lowliness is also an interior disposition: she refuses to allow her election by God to make her feel that she is elite. It is God who is great because it is God who has offered her salvation. With

> Recall a time when you became aware of God's action on your behalf. Did you learn anything about humility as a result?

the upcoming birth of her son, God's offer and power to accomplish salvation will extend to all.

Typically in prayer, we call upon God using names or descriptions that reflect our experience of God. In verse 49, Mary calls God the "Mighty One," as when Moses reminded the people upon receiving the tablets of the law that God "has done for you those great and awesome things that your own eyes have seen" (Deut 10:21). Mary also says, "holy is his name." Probably the most profound scene in the Old Testament that proclaimed God's holiness, that sense of being set apart, was found in the call of Isaiah (Isa 6:1-8). The pregnancy of Mary will prove to be a mighty deed of God for the world, and the birth of her son a call for Mary and for us to live holy lives.

[50]"His mercy is from age to age
   to those who fear him.
[51]He has shown might with his arm,
   dispersed the arrogant of mind and heart."

The focus of Mary's prayer is now squarely on God who is both merciful and mighty. What is the "fear" that counts us among those who receive God's mercy? Not to be confused with being frightened, the fear of God is to be in awe of God's power, and to revere God's presence.

The psalmist prays, "The fear of the LORD is pure, / enduring forever" (Ps 19:10), and "The fear of the LORD is the beginning of wisdom" (Ps 111:10). To fear God is to be put in right relationship with God so that our deeds reflect that disposition of awe and reverence.

Praising God's deeds in the past is not meant to be a history lesson but a testimony that God will continue to act in this way "from age to age." God's mighty acts in Israel's history are numerous but the key event is always called to mind: God overturned Pharaoh's power with an outstretched arm (see Exod 6:6; Deut 7:18-19; Isa 63:12).

In the Canticle of Mary, we focus on how God dispersed (and will disperse) the "arrogant of mind and heart." Proverbs teaches that "Every proud heart is an abomination to the LORD" (16:5) and that "Haughtiness brings humiliation, / but the humble of spirit acquire honor" (29:23). This is surely a reversal of fortunes that will continue to be a theme of Jesus' ministry, especially in the Gospel of Luke, where the theme is echoed in the words of Simeon to Mary (2:34): "this child is destined for the fall and rise of many in Israel."

Why is it important for us as a community to remember God's acts in previous generations? How do we do this in our tradition?

⁵²He has thrown down the rulers from their
    thrones
  but lifted up the lowly.
⁵³The hungry he has filled with good things;
  the rich he has sent away empty.

What is good news for many sounds very frightening or discouraging for others. The world teaches that political power and wealth are worthy goals and offer an assurance of status. The Gospel, here in the words of Mary's prayer, teaches that the hungry and the lowly are filled and lifted up.

Mary herself embodies those whose fortunes will be assured by God's special care. Without a doubt, this reversal of fortune is directed at institutional or systemic transformation as well. Genuine power creates an atmosphere where people can be truly human, respected and dignified, rather than manipulated. This is an economic reversal and it can be a frightening prospect depending on where we have placed our trust.

The beatitudes and woes of Luke's gospel (6:20-26) reinforce this message, making it clear that the kingdom of God belongs to the poor, the hungry, the weeping, and those who are hated and insulted. Mary's prayer and Jesus' teaching are consistently reminding listeners that God sees not as we see, that God measures success differently than our culture, and that God views power and wealth as a tool for attending to those who are on the fringes. This is part of what it means to be a disciple.

Sometimes it is difficult to relate to being poor or lowly, or challenging to acknowledge this in a culture that values success and achievement. What helps you to discover your own poverty? Or to relate to the physical poverty in the lives of others?

How are you an instrument of God's blessing in the lives of those who have little?

Identifying what it means to be hungry is part of the challenge for every generation who prays the *Magnificat*. Those who are indeed without food know their hunger on a very basic level, but how do we relate if we have fairly immediate access to groceries and the ability to buy on credit? Actual hunger is often not in our range of experiences. We might focus on the hungers of the human heart and mind, the hunger for meaning or truth or love, and these indeed open us to God's life. However, we might miss the economic reversal if we only look at our spiritual or emotional hungers. Getting rid of the clutter in our lives, actually and figuratively, might help us recognize our own hungers and pay closer attention to the causes of hunger throughout our world.

> When are you most aware of physical hunger? Spiritual hunger?

54"He has helped Israel his servant,
>   remembering his mercy,
55according to his promise to our fathers,
>   to Abraham and to his descendants forever."

What does it mean to speak of God remembering his mercy? First of all, the word translated as mercy is in Hebrew, the word *hesed*, which can also be translated as "faithful love" or "loving-kindness." In Scripture, mercy is not about feeling sorry for someone or some situation; mercy is about doing the loving thing. God has consistently done the loving thing with regard to Israel—liberating, shaping, entering into covenant, admonishing, and forgiving.

God remembers his mercy not by having to be reminded, but by once again, and with fervor, renewing his commitment to the people. From the womb of young Mary, through her joyful "yes" to God's plan, his own Son will usher in the kingdom of God.

Mary's words are a proclamation that God is with his people and that what God has promised is worthy of trust. The prayer began with an awareness of what God was doing within her and ends with an invitation to see that what God is doing is a fulfillment of expectations for all people.

Praying the Word / Sacred Reading

If you were to write a canticle to God, how would you focus your praise? Spend some time reflecting on that idea and then, if inclined, write your personal canticle. You may want to use one of the canticles in Luke as a model or create your own format.

Living the Word

Investigate the opportunities in your own community to learn about groups who do not have political or economic clout. How might you invest yourself in helping give a voice to the voiceless? Are there organizations that help to honor the poor and hungry, groups that offer practical assistance, and even training for new opportunities?

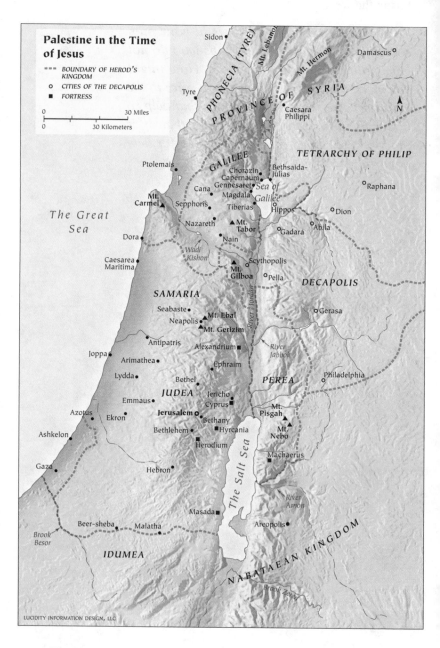

Palestine in the Time of Jesus

--- BOUNDARY OF HEROD'S KINGDOM
○ CITIES OF THE DECAPOLIS
■ FORTRESS

0   30 Miles
0   30 Kilometers

Sidon

Mt. Lebanon

Damascus ○

PHONECIA (TYRE)

Tyre ●

PROVINCE OF SYRIA

Mt. Hermon

Caesara Philippi ○

TETRARCHY OF PHILIP

GALILEE

Ptolemais ●

Chorazin ●
Capernaum ●
Cana ●
Gennesaret ●
Sepphoris ●

Bethsaida-Julias ●

Sea of Galilee

○ Raphana

Mt. Carmel ▲

Magdala ●
Tiberias ●

Hippos ○

○ Dion

The Great Sea

Nazareth ●

▲ Mt. Tabor

○ Gadara

Abila ○

Dora ●

Nain ●

Scythopolis ●

Wadi Kishon

▲ Mt. Gilboa

○ Pella

DECAPOLIS

Caesarea Maritima ●

SAMARIA

Seabaste ●
Neapolis ●

▲ Mt. Ebal
▲ Mt. Gerizim

○ Gerasa

Antipatris ●

Alexandrium ■

River Jabbok

Joppa ●

Arimathea ●

Ephraim ●

PEREA

Lydda ●

Bethel ●

Philadelphia ○

JUDEA

Emmaus ●

Jericho ●
Cyprus ■

Azotus ●

Ekron ●

Jerusalem ○
Bethany ●

Mt. Pisgah ▲

Ashkelon ●

Bethlehem ●
Hyrcania ■

Mt. Nebo ▲

Herodium ■

Machaerus ■

Gaza ●

Hebron ●

The Salt Sea

River Arnon

Masada ■

Areopolis ●

NABATAEAN KINGDOM

Beer-sheba ●
Malatha ●

Brook Besor

IDUMEA

Brook Zered

River Jordan

LUCIDITY INFORMATION DESIGN, LLC

40